Natural Disasters

Earthquakes

Louise Park

A+

Smart Apple Media

This edition first published in 2008 in the United States of America by Smart Apple Media.

Smart Apple Media
2140 Howard Drive West
North Mankato, Minnesota 56003

First published in 2007 by
MACMILLAN EDUCATION AUSTRALIA PTY LTD
627 Chapel Street, South Yarra, Australia 3141

Visit our Web site at www.macmillan.com.au or go directly to www.macmillanlibrary.com.au

Associated companies and representatives throughout the world.

Library of Congress Cataloging-in-Publication Data

Park, Louise, 1961-
  Earthquakes / by Louise Park.
  p. cm. – (Natural disasters)
  Includes index.
  ISBN 978-1-59920-111-5
1. Earthquakes–Juvenile literature. 2. Natural disasters–Juvenile literature. I. Title.

  QE521.3.P37 2007
  551.22–dc22

                                              2007004657

Edited by Sam Munday and Erin Richards
Text and cover design by Ivan Finnegan, iF design
Page layout by Ivan Finnegan, iF design
Photo research by Jes Senbergs
Illustrations by Andy Craig and Nives Porcellato, pp. 9, 10, 11, 14, 15, 16, 25
Maps by designscope, pp. 6, 12, 18, 22, 26

Printed in U.S.

Acknowledgements

The author and the publisher are grateful to the following for permission to reproduce copyright material:
Front cover photograph: collapsed building after Pakistan earthquake, October 2005, courtesy of Alamy.

Background textures courtesy of Ivan Finnegan, iF design.

AusAid/Robin Davies, pp. 26, 27; AusAid/Gregory Takats, pp. 1, 7; Marty Bahamonde/FEMA photo, p. 28; Bettmann/Corbis, pp. 18, 19;
Corbis, p. 20; EERC-NISEE,University of California, Berkeley, pp. 23 (both); Hulton Archive/Getty Images, p. 13; NGDS, pp. 12, 22, 24;
Michael Nielsen/MSF, p. 8; Stefan Pleger/MSF, p. 29; John Shea/FEMA News Photo, p. 21; Bruno Stevens/Cosmos/MSF, pp. 5, 6; Bruno
Stevens/MSF, p. 4.

Contents

GLOSSARY WORDS
When a word is printed in **bold**, you can look up its meaning in the glossary on page 31.

Natural disasters

Natural disasters are events that occur naturally. They are not caused by human action. They can happen all over the world at any time. When natural disasters occur in populated areas, they can result in death, injury, and damage to property.

Types of natural disasters

There are many types of natural disasters, such as tornadoes, wildfires, droughts, and earthquakes. Each type occurs for very different reasons and affects the Earth in different ways. Although they are different, they all create chaos and bring **devastation** and destruction with them wherever they strike.

People salvage what they can after an earthquake reduces buildings to rubble.

Earthquakes

Earthquakes are natural disasters. In the last 100 years, earthquakes have claimed the lives of hundreds of thousands of people. The damage they cause can be devastating. Earthquakes are a natural part of Earth, but what are they?

A car is crushed by part of a building that collapsed during the 2005 Pakistan earthquake.

What is an earthquake?

An earthquake is when Earth's **crust** begins to shake and vibrate. This happens when pressure and high temperatures build up deep within Earth and cause the crust to move. We do not usually feel this movement. However, sometimes the pressure becomes so great that an enormous amount of energy is released. That is when things really start to shake and a serious earthquake begins.

DISASTER FILE

Pakistan

WHAT	The deadliest earthquake of 2005
WHERE	Pakistan
WHEN	October 8, 2005
MAGNITUDE	7.6
DEPTH	16 miles (26 km)

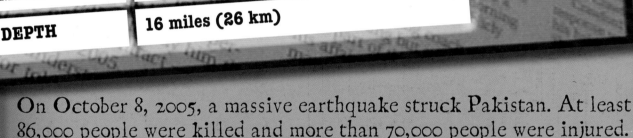

On October 8, 2005, a massive earthquake struck Pakistan. At least 86,000 people were killed and more than 70,000 people were injured. The earthquake collapsed mountains and destroyed waterways. It wiped out roads and highways. The most damage occurred in the Kashmir area, where entire villages were completely destroyed. Many other towns lost up to 80 percent of their buildings and homes.

Why did it happen?

This earthquake happened because Kashmir lies in the area where the Eurasian and Indian **tectonic plates** collide. The geological activity of these two plates causes instability in the area. The movement in 2005 caused many landslides and rockfalls. These destroyed many mountain roads and highways.

Streets were filled with rubble in the aftermath of the earthquake,

Counting the cost

The area where the Pakistan earthquake struck was very populated. As a result, it caused a lot of damage. Buildings were destroyed, lives were lost, and amenities such as electricity and water were cut off. The earthquake left close to 4 million people homeless. At least 2 million of these people are thought to be children.

Rescue and relief

The Pakistan earthquake prompted a global rescue and relief response. However, many villages were left without help for days, because rescue teams found it very difficult to get to them. Assistance came from groups and countries all over the world and helped many people survive the earthquake.

Although some buildings were left standing after the earthquake, others were completely destroyed.

SANGAM HOTEL

Earth's layers

Inside Earth there are three main layers. They are the crust, the **mantle**, and the **core**.

The crust

The outermost surface layer of Earth is called the crust. It is the most brittle layer, which is why it often cracks during an earthquake. The crust is only about 44 miles (70 km) thick and is made of cold rock.

The mantle

The mantle is the thickest of the three layers. It starts just below the crust and extends to Earth's core. The mantle is made of hot rock. Some parts are so hot that the rock has melted. This thick, **molten** substance is called magma.

Think about it

The Pakistan earthquake happened 16 miles (26 km) below the surface. This is quite shallow for an earthquake. So much powerful energy was released so close to the surface that the shaking was more violent and more devastation occurred as a result.

The violent shaking of Earth's crust during the Pakistan earthquake caused the complete collapse of many buildings.

8

The core

Below the mantle is Earth's core. It has two layers:

- the outer core
- the inner core

The core is made of metal. The outer core contains iron that is so hot that it is liquid. The inner core is even hotter yet it seems solid. This is because the pressure from all the other layers pushes the inner core into a tight lump that cannot move anywhere.

Earth's crust is the thinnest layer and the most brittle.

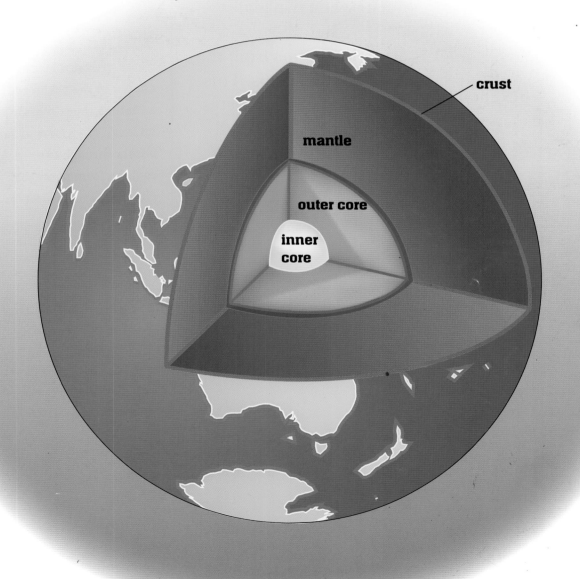

Tectonic plates

Tectonic plates are large pieces of rock that make up Earth's crust. There are seven major tectonic plates. They are very rigid and always moving as they float on the magma that flows through the mantle. As the magma flows underneath them, it pushes the plates and causes them to bump and rub together. Most earthquakes occur along the edges, or boundaries, of these tectonic plates. There are three types of plate boundaries. Each one has a different way of moving and causes a different type of earthquake.

Divergent boundaries

Divergent boundaries occur when two plates move away from each other. When the plates move apart, a crack is created. Magma from the mantle swells up into the crack and cools. This creates more crust in the ocean floor. As plates move further apart and more crust is created, the ocean floor expands. This is known as seafloor spreading.

Think about it

There are huge mountain chains in the ocean that are as tall as the mountain chains on land. They form as magma bursts through the crack and cools to form new crust on either side of the crack.

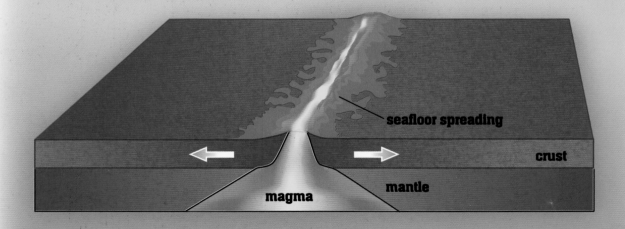

Tectonic plates move away from each other at divergent boundaries.

seafloor spreading

crust

mantle

magma

Convergent boundaries

Convergent boundaries occur when one plate slides over the top of another. The zone where the two plates meet is called the subduction zone. Very strong earthquakes happen at the site of convergent boundaries. The lower plate gets pushed down into the hot magma and starts to melt.

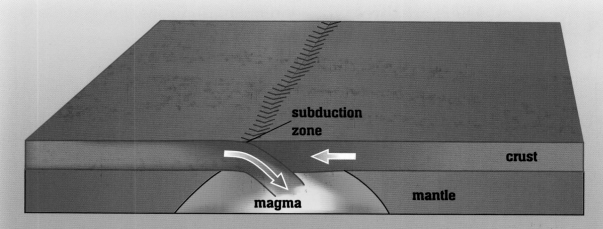

At convergent boundaries, two plates meet and force one on top of the other.

Transform boundaries

Transform boundaries occur when two plates slide past each other. The buildup and release of strain as the plates slide produce earthquakes. Sometimes the plates cause so much stress that they break and create gaps known as faults. These gaps cannot be closed.

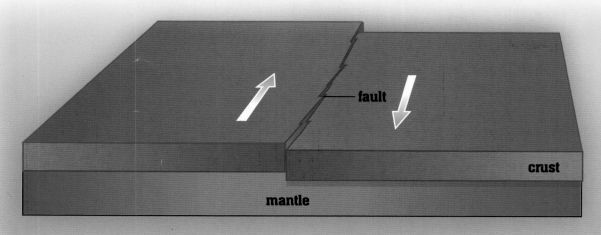

At transform boundaries, two plates grind past each other.

DISASTER FILE
San Andreas Fault

WHAT	The San Andreas Fault
WHERE	Northern California to Southern California, United States
LENGTH	More than 800 miles (1,287 km)
DEPTH	More than 10 miles (16 km)

What is the San Andreas Fault?

The San Andreas Fault exists where two moving plates, the Pacific Plate and the North American Plate, meet. It is a transform boundary and a continuous break in Earth's crust. Because blocks of rock on opposite sides of the fault move horizontally in different directions, the two sides do not line up. At one section of the fault, the difference in height between the two sides has been measured at more than 150 miles (241 km)!

Think about it

During the San Francisco earthquake in 1906, a road was split by one side moving to the right by more than 0 feet (6 m). That is the highest shift ever recorded.

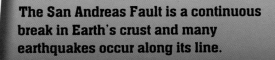

The San Andreas Fault is a continuous break in Earth's crust and many earthquakes occur along its line.

Earthquakes along the San Andreas Fault

The most significant disaster to occur along the fault in Northern California was the earthquake of April 18, 1906. The rupture along the fault was 296 miles (477 km) long. The first shocks were felt at about 5 A.M. local time throughout the San Francisco Bay area. The earthquake followed about 30 seconds later. Violent shocks and strong shaking lasted for about a minute.

As a result of this earthquake, 3,000 people died and up to 300,000 were left homeless. The earthquake and its aftershocks caused a great deal of damage. However, the most damage was caused by the fires that burned out of control afterwards, destroying 28,000 buildings. It has been estimated that about 90 percent of the total destruction was done by fires.

Think about it

Studies have shown that very large earthquakes occur along the southern section of the San Andreas Fault about every 150 years. With the la[st] one occurring in 1857, that means another big one is d[ue] there very soon!

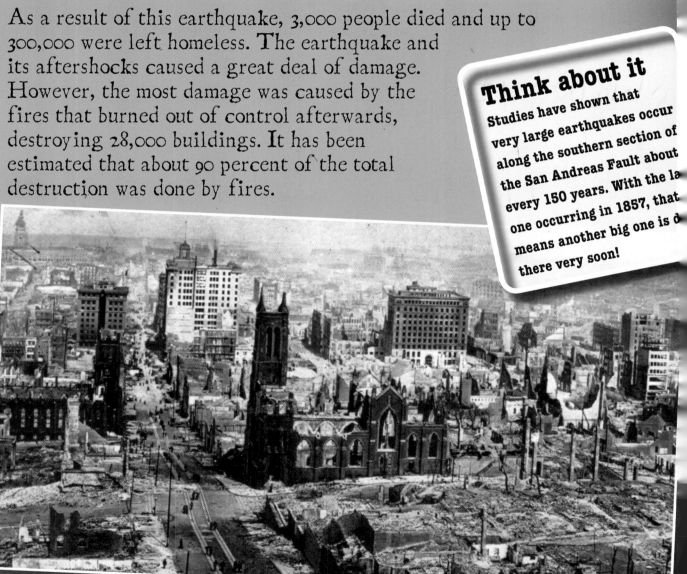

The 1906 San Francisco earthquake destroyed hundreds of buildings.

During an earthquake

During an earthquake, tectonic plates move against each other with great force. This force creates an enormous amount of stress. Stress creates strain within the rocks and can cause them to shorten, lengthen, pull apart, or slip past each other. Eventually, so much stress and energy is released that the rocks snap suddenly. This causes huge amounts of shaking and vibration. The energy released during this process is called seismic energy. This energy travels through Earth in waves, known as seismic waves. There are different types of seismic waves and each type has a different result.

Primary waves

Primary waves are the first waves of an earthquake. They travel more quickly than any other kind of wave. These waves can travel through solid, liquid, and gas. As they travel through rock, the waves move tiny rock particles in a squeeze and release motion. These waves typically arrive at the surface as a noise or rumble.

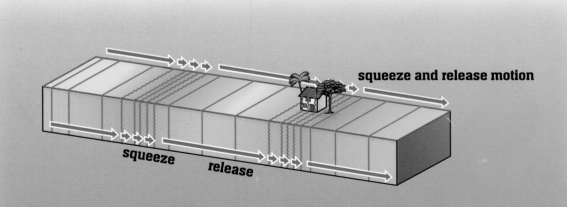

Primary waves travel quickly through Earth.

Shear waves

Primary waves are followed by shear waves. These waves shake and wobble the ground from side to side. These waves cause the first rolling along the surface that happens during an earthquake. Shear waves do not move through everything. They only travel through solid material.

side to side motion

Shear waves shake the ground from side to side.

Surface waves

Surface waves ripple along the surface of Earth like waves of water. Surface waves are the deadliest of all the seismic waves. They can turn the ground beneath your feet into waves that roll and crash as if you were surfing. This wave effect causes buildings to collapse and roads to split.

Think about it

The energy released from an earthquake can be the same as setting off millions of tons of explosives at once. An earthquake is capable of giving off more energy than the nuclear bomb that was dropped on Hiroshima in Japan in 1945.

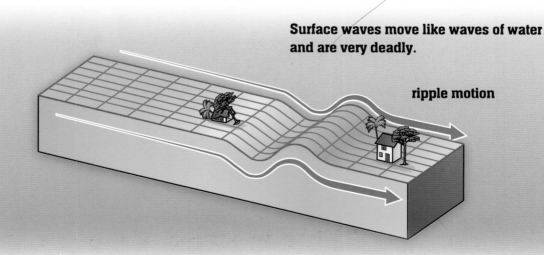

Surface waves move like waves of water and are very deadly.

ripple motion

15

Measuring an earthquake

Scientists use special instruments to locate and measure an earthquake. They can locate the area inside Earth where the earthquake starts, called the focus. They can also locate the area on Earth's surface where the earthquake is most strongly felt, called the epicenter.

The focus

The focus of an earthquake can be as deep as 373 miles (600 km) underground. Sometimes the focus is shallow and released within the crust itself. Seismic waves travel out in all directions from the focus. They move through Earth, travel down into it, and travel up to the surface, where the waves are at their strongest. The farther they travel, the weaker the waves become.

The epicenter

The point on Earth's surface directly above the focus is called the epicenter. It is at this point that the strongest shock waves are felt. The most damage and destruction occurs at and near the epicenter of an earthquake.

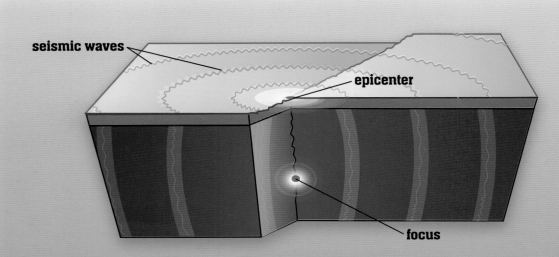

seismic waves

epicenter

focus

When energy is released during an earthquake, it travels up from the focus to the epicenter and travels outward in all directions.

Seismographs

Scientists measure an earthquake by recording and studying the seismic energy it releases. They do this by using a tool called a seismograph. Seismographs pick up the vibrations and seismic energy coming from the earthquake and record them as a wavy line. Scientists operate seismographs all over the world and often work together to locate an earthquake's epicenter. It takes three or more seismographs to do this. One seismograph can only tell how far the earthquake is from itself, so it takes several seismographs in different locations to get accurate information.

The Richter scale

Scientists use a grading system, called the Richter scale, to measure the **magnitude** of an earthquake. Each number on the scale represents an earthquake that is ten times more powerful than the number before it. Earthquakes that measure below 3 are generally not felt. Any earthquake measuring 5 or more on the Richter scale is likely to cause the loss of lives.

RICHTER SCALE

Magnitude	Potential damage	Description
less than 3	none	• generally not felt, rarely any damage
3–3.9	minimal	• felt, but often mistaken for a passing truck • dishes and other indoor items disturbed
4–5.9	moderate	• noticeable shaking • furniture moves, windows break • poorly built buildings severely damaged • slight damage to other buildings
6–6.9	severe	• poorly built buildings destroyed • moderate damage to other buildings • chimneys and walls may collapse
7–7.9	extreme	• all buildings suffer major damage • cracks in the ground • foundations shift, structures destroyed • landslides may occur
8+	catastrophic	• surface waves can be seen • bridges collapse • wide cracks in the ground • objects thrown into the air • almost all structures destroyed

DISASTER FILE
Chile

WHAT	The most powerful earthquake ever recorded
WHERE	Eastern Pacific Ocean, off the coast of Chile, South America
WHEN	1960
MAGNITUDE	9.5
DEPTH	37 miles (60 km)

The most powerful earthquake ever recorded hit Chile in 1960. It had a magnitude of 9.5 on the Richter scale. Its epicenter was 197 feet (60 m) below the ocean floor, so Chile suffered strong seismic sea waves as well as strong seismic waves through the earth. This earthquake caused a **tsunami**.

Why did it happen?

The Chilean earthquake occurred because an area of the seafloor known as the Nazca Plate slid about 50 feet (15 m) under the continent of South America. This **offshore** part of the continent snapped upward like a spring, releasing enormous amounts of seismic energy. This massive movement of the ocean floor moved the sea above it, which caused the tsunami.

Many houses survived the earthquake, but were destroyed by the tsunami which followed.

Counting the cost

Most of the damage from the Chilean earthquake was actually caused by the tsunami. The tsunami raced across the ocean, hitting Chile, Hawaii, Japan, the Philippines, and the west coast of the U.S. In Chile, the earthquake and the tsunami that followed took more than 2,000 lives and caused severe property damage. The tsunami also killed 61 people in Hawaii and 122 in Japan.

This earthquake did not only cause damage to man-made structures. Earth itself was changed forever. Huge landslides and **debris** flows were sent tumbling down mountain slopes. Some of these landslides were so big they changed the course of rivers. Some were dammed up completely.

DID YOU KNOW?

When this earthquake happene seismographs recorded seismic that traveled all around Earth. Th shook the whole Earth for days.

Fishing boats sheltering in Hachinohe Harbor, Japan, were tossed about by the deadly tsunami.

Liquefaction and avalanches

The shaking of Earth is not the only way that damage can occur during an earthquake. Sometimes **liquefaction** and **avalanches** can cause even greater damage than the earthquake itself.

Liquefaction

Sometimes an earthquake can change the very ground we walk on. Some ground surfaces are made of loosely-packed sand and gravel. When an earthquake shakes this kind of surface, it can force underground water to rise and mix with it. This process is known as liquefaction, and it turns the ground into a liquid similar to quicksand. When this occurs, anything built on that soil will sink and collapse. Liquefaction is often responsible for damage to property and buildings.

DID YOU KNOW?

The world's deadliest earthquake happened in China in 1556. The earthquake hit an area where most people lived in caves built into cliffs. The cliffs collapsed and buried an estimated 83,000 people.

These buildings are sinking because the liquid soil cannot hold their weight anymore.

Landslides and avalanches

The sudden shaking from an earthquake can cause rocks, soil, and snow to fall and slide from mountains, known as landslides and avalanches. Landslides and avalanches can occur in a wide variety of environments, even underwater. The huge amount of debris involved can be extremely destructive.

Landslides and avalanches can do an enormous amount of damage.

Underwater landslides

Underwater landslides can do just as much damage as those above ground. They commonly occur when one tectonic plate is lifted up while another one slides underneath it. The lift in the plate creates a mountain in the seafloor. The seafloor slides down the slope just like an avalanche on a mountain above ground, causing the same sort of damage.

HAT	The worst avalanche ever recorded
HERE	Peru
WHEN	On May 31, 1970
MAGNITUDE	8.1
AVALANCHE LENGTH	262 feet (80 m)

On 31 May 1970, Southern Peru experienced a huge earthquake. It occurred along the subduction zone between the Nazca Plate and the South American Plate. This earthquake triggered the worst avalanche disaster ever recorded.

The huge avalanche started from the **summit** of Nevado de Huascarán, an extinct volcano. Nevado de Huascarán is the highest mountain in Peru. From this summit, a wall of ice was dislodged and within three minutes it had slid down a glacier. The debris from this fall traveled another 6 miles (10 km) and buried the town of Yungay.

The Peru avalanche was so deadly because the debris traveled such a long distance, gaining speed all the time.

Why did it happen?

This avalanche was triggered by an earthquake that lasted just 60 seconds. The earthquake dislodged millions of tons of icy snow from the high slopes of Nevado de Huascarán. The wall of ice fell into lakes and reservoirs, causing them to overflow. This created a wave of mud, ice, debris, and rocks. This avalanche slipped down the mountain at 250 miles (402 km) an hour, toward populated areas.

Counting the cost

This avalanche buried the towns of Yungay and Ranrahirca completely. The estimated death toll from the earthquake and avalanche was 6,000. Around 20,000 people went missing and over 500,000 people were left homeless. The earthquake and avalanche destroyed about 200,000 homes and buildings and wiped out entire settlements.

YUNGAY ANTES

This is an aerial view of Yungay before the landslide.

AQUI ESTUVO YUNGAY
(25,000 habitantes)

X

PLAZA DE ARMAS

The deadly avalanche completely buried the town of Yungay.

Floods and tsunamis

Earthquakes often cause floods and tsunamis. These water disasters frequently kill more people than the earthquake itself.

Floods

Earthquakes can cause falling rocks and mud to tumble into lakes and rivers, making them overflow and flood the surrounding areas. Earthquakes can also break dams, causing the water to escape.

Tsunamis

Tsunamis are seismic sea waves, caused by movements along faults and undersea landslides. These powerful waves can travel thousands of miles across the ocean and bring damage to countries far away.

The tsunami caused by the Chile earthquake bent parking meters over when it hit the coast of Hawaii.

Think about it

After the earthquake that struck Chile in 1960, tsunami waves traveled enormous distances. When they finally hit the coast, they were more than 20 feet (6 m) high.

Tsunami waves

Waves travel outward in all directions from where a tsunami starts, just like the ripples caused by throwing a rock into a pond. Tsunamis do not rise and curl like most ocean waves. As they move into shallow water they build and become stronger. They flood over the coast in huge surges and withdrawals, like a great wall of water.

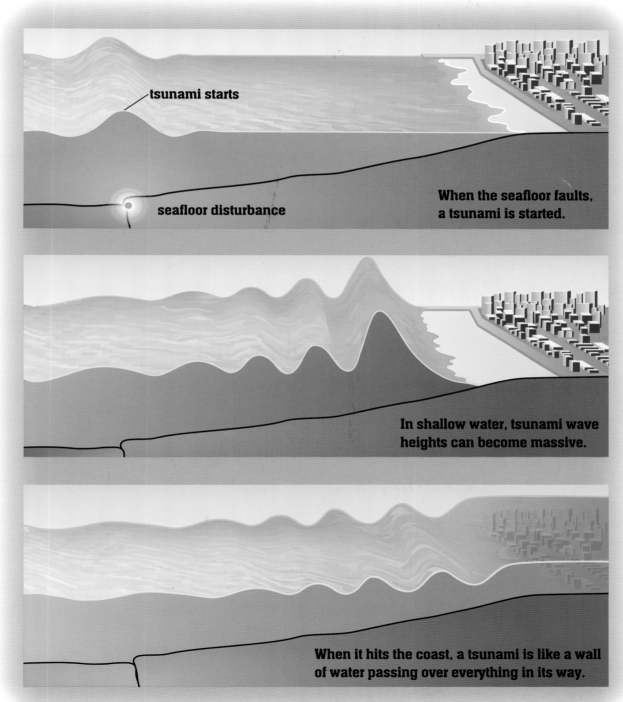

tsunami starts

seafloor disturbance

When the seafloor faults, a tsunami is started.

In shallow water, tsunami wave heights can become massive.

When it hits the coast, a tsunami is like a wall of water passing over everything in its way.

DISASTER FILE
Indian Ocean

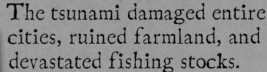

WHAT	The deadliest tsunami ever created by an earthquake
WHERE	Off the coast of Sumatra, Indonesia
WHEN	December 26, 2004
MAGNITUDE	9.0

On December 26, 2004, the largest earthquake in 40 years took place in the Indian Ocean. The earthquake triggered the deadliest tsunami in world history. It was so powerful that the waves caused devastation on the coast of Africa and were even detected on the East Coast of the U.S. Eleven countries bordering the Indian Ocean were affected. The tsunami damaged entire cities, ruined farmland, and devastated fishing stocks.

A strong earthquake lasting 20 seconds or more near the coast can generate a tsunami. This Indian Ocean undersea earthquake lasted for close to 10 minutes. It caused the entire planet to vibrate. The tsunami it created killed more than 283,100 people.

The tsunami completely destroyed many houses in Aceh, Indonesia.

Why did it happen?

There is a complex structure of tectonic plates near the island of Sumatra, Indonesia. These plates are continually grinding against each other, with the convergent boundaries causing the biggest problems. On December 26, 2004, a rupture occurred with one plate slipping underneath the other. It generated an earthquake and the tsunami that followed.

Counting the cost

Apart from the massive human death toll, it has been estimated that another 1,126,900 people lost their homes. Damage to rainforests, coral reefs, land, and vegetation was also extensive. Salt water destroyed or polluted the freshwater supplies to the area. This caused shortages of food and water and loss of livelihood.

Debris from the tsunami covered coastal areas in Aceh, Indonesia.

Disaster relief

Earthquakes cause all kinds of damage. The first step after an earthquake is to rescue any survivors. Depending on the effects of the quake, this can be an enormous task. Next, areas are set up where relief can be provided to victims. People who have suffered the effects of an earthquake may need more than medical attention. They will also need clothing, shelter, food, and fresh water.

Once relief workers have taken care of the victims, it is then time to assess the damage. The clean-up operation also begins. Dangerously damaged structures such as homes, roads, and bridges need to be demolished. Once this is done, then the rebuilding begins. The costs of rebuilding communities can be massive. This can place strain on the economy of the country and on its government. Sometimes, extensive damage attracts aid from other countries that wish to help.

Rescue workers assess the damage after an earthquake.

Global aid

Global aid plays an enormous part in disaster relief. Donations and aid are very important to any relief effort. Just six months after the 2004 Indian Ocean tsunami, countries around the world had given up to $13 billion in aid.

Living with earthquakes

As the world's population increases, so does the danger of humans suffering from earthquakes. More people will be living in earthquake-prone areas as cities become more and more populated.

Helping people understand the dangers of earthquakes will keep them safer. Knowing what to do when an earthquake happens can make all the difference when it comes to saving lives. Scientists have a key role to play in living with earthquakes. Accurate predictions and warnings mean people can be prepared when an earthquake does strike.

Aid workers flew in from all over the world to help victims of the Indian Ocean tsunami.

DISASTER FILES AT A GLANCE

The four earthquakes profiled in this book are record-breaking for different reasons. This graph shows their magnitude and their death tolls.

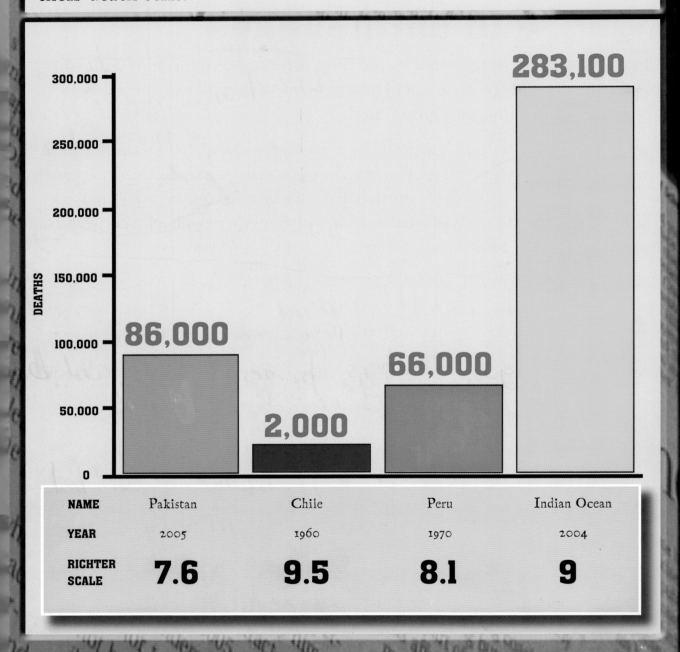

NAME	Pakistan	Chile	Peru	Indian Ocean
YEAR	2005	1960	1970	2004
RICHTER SCALE	**7.6**	**9.5**	**8.1**	**9**

Glossary

avalanches   large amounts of earth, ice, or snow that slide down a mountain

core   the center of Earth

crust   the hard surface layer of Earth

debris   the remains of things that have been broken or destroyed

devastation   severe damage or destruction

liquefaction   when soil becomes like quicksand

magnitude   the strength or size of an earthquake

mantle   layer of hot rock beneath Earth's crust

molten   made liquid by heat

offshore   located a distance from the shore

summit   the very top of a mountain

tectonic plates   large plates of rock that make up Earth's crust

tsunami   a huge wave caused by a disturbance in the ocean floor

Index